Piled Higher and Deeper
on the Cariboo Trail

W. Ciddle, cci

Piled Higher and Deeper on the Cariboo Trail

Poetry by Mike Puhallo
Cartoons by Wendy Liddle

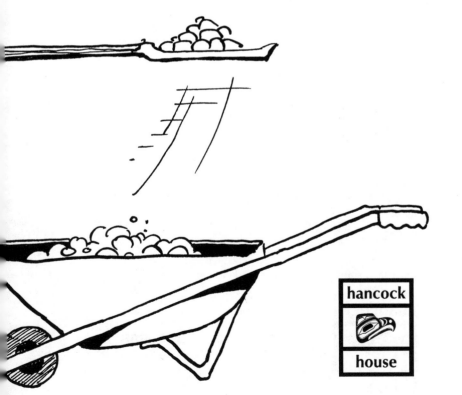

hancock
house

ISBN 0-88839-487-X

Cataloging in Publication Data
Puhallo, Mike, 1953–
    Piled higher and deeper on the Cariboo trail

    Poems.
    ISBN 0-88839-487-X

    1. Cowboys—Poetry. 2. Ranch life—Poetry.
3. Cariboo Region (B.C.)—Poetry. I. Liddle, Wendy.
II. Title.
PS8581.U42P54 2001   C811'.54   C2001-910473-1
PR9199.3.P77P54 2001

Editor: Rick Rogers
Production: Nondus L. Douglas, Ingrid Luters
Cover art: Wendy Liddle

*We acknowledge the financial support of the Government of Canada
through the Book Publishing Industry Development Program (BPIDP)
for our publishing activities.*

Published simultaneously in Canada and the United States by

HANCOCK HOUSE PUBLISHERS LTD.
19313 Zero Avenue, Surrey, B.C. V3S 9R9

HANCOCK HOUSE PUBLISHERS
1431 Harrison Avenue, Blaine, WA 98230-5005

(604) 538-1114   Fax (604) 538-2262
(800) 938-1114   Fax (800) 983-2262
Web Site: www.hancockhouse.com   *email:* sales@hancockhouse.com

Contents

Preface

Cowboy poetry may be new to a lot of folks, but it has been around at least as long as there have been cowboys. Some of my poems have historical roots, some are just good ol' BS stories that kind of rhyme. Some are sort of true and some come right out of the blue. I do make a serious effort never to let the truth get in the way of a good story.

Friends are pulling into town
to swap some yarns and rhymes.
Sing some songs and reminisce,
about them good ol' Cowboy times.

The misery of pulling calves,
when it's thirty-five below.
The summer droughts,
the rain-soaked trails,
cold winds and driftin' snow.

Gosh! It sounds romantic,
when ranch life's put to rhyme.
Then, there's all those funny stories...
That didn't seem so at the time.

All things being equal...
right down to slim paychecks,
I'd rather tell the stories,
and let my brother have the wrecks!

A special dedication and thanks go to Linda for putting up with my particular brand of insanity, to Wendy Liddle for interpreting it so well in her drawings and, of course, to her husband Mark for allowing her to work with me!

Sun Baked Meadow Muffins

Ah yes, it is finally summer, the time of year when a pile of fresh BS or a green cow patty, quickly matures into a dry, sanitary MEADOW MUFFIN.

A meadow muffin is a marvelous thing,
The kind of BS that's fun to fling.
For when the chips are down, and good and dry.
Like organic frisbees they can fly!

Now to a bug, it's home sweet home,
and it's fertilizer to clover and brome.
As for the muffin man, there ain't no doubt,
my humor's better, when the Sun comes out!

In the Beginning

Back when three-toed Eohippus,
pulled Apollo across the sky,
The first cowboy crawled out of his bedroll
to give that bronc a try.
To this day scientists are still hunting for ol' Link
Searching high and low to find his bones.
But a mite too high, I think!
I figure that first human,
must have been about three foot tall,
It only stands to reason,
if their horses was so small!

August Nights

August nights are special,
with the smell of fresh cut hay.
When the moon is down
the ebony sky
shows off the Milky Way.
To wish upon a falling star
for whatever your heart's delight.
The best time is now,
for meteor showers
often grace an August night.
I've always been a night owl,
and on each falling star I sight,
I wish for a few less mosquitoes
sharing this August night!

A Time to Catch Your Breath

(November)

I rode through the cows on the Meadow today,
and pulled the horse's shoes,
We might get snow later on this week,
according to the news.

November is a quiet month,
On the Chilcotin Range,
With most things ready for winter,
there's time to relax for a change.

I kind of like this time of year,
all the machinery is put away,
the calves are shipped, the fences fixed,
and we're not yet feeding hay.

A Cowboy's Winter Wish

(December)

The heifer calves are fat as jelly beans,
It's another fine fall day.
I don't know just where winter went,
but I hope it stays away
because I don't own no snowmobile,
and I never learned to ski.
So if the weather's mild and the snow don't come,
that's quite all right with me.
Now that it's December
I focus on one thing,
the longer winter stays away,
the sooner comes the Spring!

Christmas Shopping

I read an article the other day, where some "Einstein" with a Ph.D. had been doing research about the stress of Christmas shopping. Now we all know that stress is the major cause of every disease from heart attacks and strokes to calf scours. The most interesting statistic coming out of all this was that women suffered less from this seasonal malady than men. This was considered remarkable in light of the fact that women actually do most of the Christmas shopping! What I find remarkable is that a psychologist who went to school all those years, can't figure out that most women regard shopping as a form of recreation! This project was probably funded by your tax dollars.

I gassed up my old pick-up,
and headed into town.
about the only time I go to a mall,
is when Christmas rolls around.
This ol' Cowboy feels so out of place,
and all them folks are rushing so.
I've got to find that special gift,
but I ain't sure where to go.
I saw a lot of stuff we can't afford,
as I wandered up and down.
Then I remembered a little shop
on the other side of town.
Now some folks call that old stuff junk,
but they're wrong as they can be.
Besides I know she's fond of old antiques,
or she would not have married me.

Fresh Horses

The old year has been turned
   out to pasture, and it's
   time to start anew,
So let's run this new year in
   the pen and see what she
   can do!
She might look a little spooky,
   but that should not phase us none.
'Cause the last few years were all kinda
   rank, back when they was
   young.
But we rode through every twist
   and turn we met along the way.
And settled all our squabbles
   without clubs or pepper spray.
There ain't much we can't handle,
   'though we ain't boastful loud or crude.
All it takes is a little try,
   and some cowboy attitude.
Now I ain't saying it will be easy,
   and there's bound to be some wrecks.
But cowboys thrive on challenges,
   hard times and slim paychecks!
So check your cinch and step aboard,
   never mind the warnings.
I pray I never get too old,
   for fresh colts and frosty mornings!

Happy New Year!

Twilight Ranch Branding

To pitch in and help at branding time,
is a tradition of the Range.
But how far some travel to share our work,
might seem a little strange.
Now ol' Dave is from Saskatchewan,
a cowboy born and raised.
But now on the west coast on a movie set,
is where he spends most days.
Friend Jack comes from Montana
just to help us rope and brand.
These are just a pair of a dozen or more,
who come to lend a lend.
We've had artists, athletes and writers,
And friends who work in town.
It might be registered nurse
or a rodeo queen
Holding that calf on the ground.
A day of sweat, dust and smoke
bawling cows and burning hair
and worth the trip anytime
Just to see who else is there!

A Full Moon in April

Green grass and budding trees,
the damp-earth smell of springtime
on a gentle southern breeze.
We walk the river's edge
by moonlight
some wild geese
swim nearby.
Black shapes
on silver water.
We hear their wary cry.
My horses graze in the meadow,
beneath the same moonlit sky.
Do you suppose they're aware,
of its splendor
or is it a secret,
between you
and I.

Since Robert Redford made that movie, every Jack-ass that owns a sad-
dle seems to think he is some kind of horse whisperer. Yes, natural
horsemanship works; it has for centuries. There have been great strides
made in training methods, training riders to be better horsemen. But
there have always been some whose gift, defies explanation.

The Sacred Orb

All the secrets of the ages,
Every thing between earth and sky,
Has been reflected in that Crystal Orb,
That is a horse's eye.

It was the legacy of the old ones,
closely guarded ancient lore.
The magic bond between man and beast,
In work, sport and war.

Treat the gift not lightly,
It was Alexander's vein,
The strength of Genghis Khan,
Arthur, and Charlemagne.

Basques, Celts, Afghanis,
And all those dusky desert tribes.
Among the landless, restless nations,
The *Knowing* long has thrived.

To look into an equine eye,
and read what's written there
Is a gift few mortal men still know,
and fewer still would share.

All the secrets of the ages,
Every thing between earth and sky,
Has been reflected in that Crystal Orb,
That is a horse's eye.

Cowboy Pride

A cowboy's pride and honor,
won't let him give much ground.
He can lead, or he can follow,
but he can't be pushed around!

Sneak Attack

A pretty young lady drove in the yard,
just the other day.
I was sweating an' cursing trying to tack a shoe,
on my brother's spooky grey.
It was a good excuse to rest a bit,
and see what this woman wanted.
The questions she asked, and things she said,
gave me chills, and left me haunted!
It seems she was hired to review the assessments,
of farms and ranches on this route.
To make sure we was paying our share of taxes,
as near as I could make out.
She explained to me the different farm classes,
and the appropriate rates of tax.
I was beginning to get a bit concerned,
by the way she laid out the facts.
It seems the Government don't give a damn,
if farmers is in a fix.
Looks to me like it's just part of a plan
—the dirtiest lowest of tricks.
Because if you take on a job,
to cover your bills,
and keep the banker at bay,
they'll call farmin' your hobby,
change your assessment,
and double the taxes you pay!

Ode to Robbie Burns

Och Robbie, how your verse and rhyme,
Try a wit and tongue like mine.
Aye, even friends of Scottish blood,
Wallow in thy lyric mud.

While some poems flow,
with rhythm plain,
Your phrases writhe in bitter pain,
of a language hacked by a bard insane!

I must struggle to read,
This tangled tome,
Of how one wee beastie,
lost his home!

Yet, due the eloquence
of simple truth,
Your words can
never die.
For the best laid plans,
O' mice and men,
do yet,
"gang aft, agley"

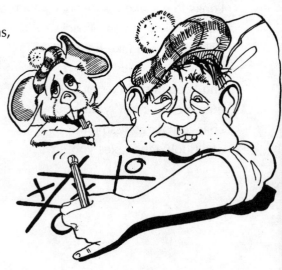

A Cowboy's Guide to
Gravity

I put shoes on my little roan mare today, and as I drove the last nail in the last shoe, she jerked her foot away and drove the nail through my finger. Did I ever tell you how much I love shoeing horses?

Jack Drake taught me about shoeing nags,
when I was just a kid.
He claimed teaching young folks to shoe horses,
WAS THE MEANEST THING HE EVER DID.

Now I don't do it for a living,
I've steered clear of that rut.
Because it can cause brain damage,
to work all day,
with your head below your Butt!

Resilience...

Is a trodden blade of grass,
though bent,
it is not broke.
A trait that's often found as well,
among ranch and farmin' folk!

Northern Lights

A silent call,
I could not sleep.
so I took a walk
by moonlight,
instead of counting sheep!

Brilliance and color,
in a cloudless sky,
held me so in awe.
As the Northern lights,
right over head,
the brightest I ever saw.

The Moon was two days shy of full,
and big as it could be.
While the mystic curtain
shimmered and danced.
A night of magic, and mystery!

Chrome Steel Cowboys

I was in Clinton recently for their Cowboy poetry night, as well as the annual gathering of a motorcycle club from the coast. The crowd at the community hall and the bunch of bikers at the campground sure did not look like they had much in common.

Performing cowboy poetry for bikers,
It sounds crazy I suppose!
Gold Wing riders and Harley Hoggers,
Enthralled by rustic prose?

One Hog rider that I spoke with,
kind of put it all in place.
"A steed of steel, like one with hooves,
lets you feel the wind on your face!"

"It depends on where you grow up,
and down which trail you start,
but every outlaw mounted on chrome steel,
is a cowboy deep at heart!"

The other day I was watching a red-tailed hawk sitting in the middle of my driveway, about a hundred yards from the house. He seemed to be smiling; well, if a hawk could smile, he would have been smiling!

Smilin'

A flicker of movement caught my eye,
as I watched that great regal hawk.
It was my wife's little cat pressed flat to the ground,
intently beginning to stalk.

Have you ever seen a hawk smile,
I assure you he did, and I'm smiling too as I think.
That if this is a sign of how intelligent they are
it's a wonder that cats ain't extinct !

What Did you Feed that Dog?

Four cowboys and a Red-Heeler dog,
off on a rodeo run.
Screamin' through the night when it's twenty below,
With all the windows undone.

Any fool knows cow dogs and pizza,
have to be kept apart!
'Cause a skunk is downright fragrant
compared to Ol' Zeke's garlic fart!

In 1998 we had one of the hottest summers and worst forest fire sea-
sons ever in the interior of British Columbia. Some folks on Vancouver
Island asked us to come down and take part in their first Cowboy Poetry
gathering. Things on the old homestead being pretty well under control,
and Linda and I being tired of the smell of smoke, we packed up the
camper and headed for the coast. We toured around a bit, saw the big
museum in Victoria and the wonderful murals at Chemainus. We made
some new friends, I recited my rhymes and as we were about to leave,
we saw something we hadn't seen in a month, CLOUDS!

28

Vancouver Island Round-up

We was on the north end of the Island,
when we spotted the first few strays.
Pards they was the prettiest thing,
I'd seen in many days.
We thought about the folks back home,
fighting forest fires and drought.
So Ma drove the camper,
while I shook my riata out.
By nightfall we had a pretty good herd,
headed up the draw.
The finest gathering of rain clouds,
anyone ever saw.
We let them water in Georgia Strait
then pushed them through the night.
So when we turned them loose at Cherry Creek,
our timing was just right!
The fires was out within a day,
the drought was darn sure broke,
I know this sounds like some tall tale,
but folks it ain't no joke.
Now, I know where them clouds brush up,
so if it gets real bad again.
I'll head down to the Island,
and round us up some rain.

Horse Drawn Tour

Linda and I visited Vancouver Island recently. The little town of Chemainus has almost every building decorated with beautiful murals depicting the history of the region. As we took a horse drawn tour of the city, I could not help compare the lot of the geldings pulling our wagon to the lives of their predecessors in the paintings.

Some might think it boring for
    Diamond and Pat
to plod the same rounds every day.
Their teamster turned tour guide,
chats with the passengers,
and points out the sights on the way.
This mismatched team,
A Percheron and a Clyde,
wind through traffic in streets
that ain't very wide.
They've wisely studied the murals,
along their meandering route,
and of their own good fortune,
they haven't any doubt.
A pretty blonde lady,
gently handles their reins,
as they pass by the paintings
of loggers and trains...

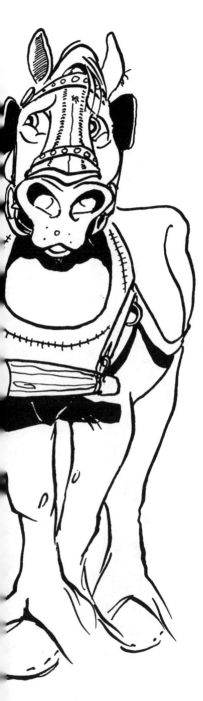

and those old time horses,
on the skid trails and roads,
pushed with curses and whips
to move impossible loads.
They strained in their harness
braving mud, heat and fire,
'till their big hearts exploded,
and they sank in the mire....

A half hour at a walk,
and this tour's at an end
and here comes young Kelly,
with water again.
Let others dream of bygone days,
the frontier life and its rowdy ways.
There's two lucky horses
    that rest in the shade,
secure in the Knowledge
that they've got it made!

The Hunter

The Highway Patrolman's out hunting,
high risk, for minimal pay.
He thrills to the roar of his engine,
as he hunts his fleet quarry all day,
and busts all the truckers and cowboys,
who happen to drive the same way!

Is This Global Warming?

*After three easy winters in a row I might be getting spoiled. I had to
keep cutting back my horses feed 'cause they were getting too fat. My
wife said the same thing about me!*

The Canada Geese are pairing off,
real early again this year.
The ice is gone from the round corral,
spring time must be near.
The willows along the river ,
are already starting to bud,
The cars and trucks around this place,
are totally covered with mud.
I don't care if it's just a cycle,
or Global Warming is the cause.
What I know for sure,
is the cows and I,
have grown fond of,
midwinter thaws!

A Cowboy's Valentine

The cows have had their vitamins,
and a shot of scour vaccine.
The medicine kit has been restocked;
the calf jack and chains are clean.

You threw out your leaky gumboots,
and bought a brand new pair.
Valentine's Day is here once more
so cowboy please take care.

If you want calving time to slip by sm
with the least amount of strife.
You'd better take this opportunity,
to be nice to your wife.

So take your darlin' dancing
and be sure to treat her right.
'Cause then she'll be far less grumpy,
about checking cows at night.

Lawnmowers

The bay mare's foal is ten days old,
a pretty sorrel filly,
it's a treat to watch her buck and play
having fun and acting silly.

Some times I leave the gate unclosed
between the yard and their small pasture.
The garden isn't up just yet
so there won't be no disaster!

From our park bench on the front porch,
we enjoy our after-dinner sit,
and watch Momma trim the front lawn
while the foal explores a bit.

Canada Is

Canada is a poet's dream,
a land so diverse and wide.
It takes a lot of imagination,
to see the other side.

I consider myself lucky,
you see I have been blessed,
with a view of this great nation,
from the high ground, way out west!

Oh! It is an awesome view,
for those who care to see,
whether you're looking at what is, or was,
or what is yet to be!

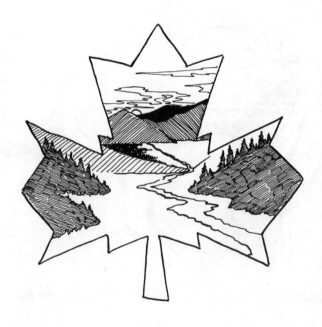

There are challenges we must face,
and divisions yet to mend.
but they're like breezes in the meadow
that cause the grass to bend.

For we are a youthful nation,
growing stronger all the while,
and our greatest tribulations,
would make our forefathers smile.

Close your eyes and share my vision,
of a nation just and free,
leading the world into a brand new age.
Just close your eyes... and see!

A Campfire Tale from the Cariboo Trail

The old-time cowboys west of the Rockies differed in many ways from those on the eastern slope. Their tack and methods of handling cattle and horses were acquired from the Vaqueros of California, who began to come north at least forty years before cattle began to move out of Texas toward Montana. The influence of the Vaquero is still evident throughout the ranch lands of the Pacific Northwest.

38

José Tressierra

My name is José Tressierra,
    best bull-wacker on the Cariboo Trail.
My wife Josephine and son Pablo
    wait for me at my cabin in Yale.

I am a man your history has forgotten.
    but Amigos, I have seen it all.
Since I left my old home in Sonora,
    where only mesquite and saguaro grow tall.

I walked to the San Joaquin Valley,
    when I was a skinny young lad.
To learn the ways of the Vaquero,
    I rode the best horses they had.

When Mcloud came south to buy cattle,
    for Douglas, the Hudson Bay boss,
we drove a thousand wild cows from the *la baranca*,
    north to the Columbia and across.

Valenzuela and I rode with a herd to Snake River,
    land of the Great Nez Percé.
We wintered our herds in that bunchgrass,
    tapedero high all the way!

Los Indios es muis bueno Caballeros,
    but they did not know much about cows!
The Scotchmen were *sabé* about cattle,
    but as horsemen, were lacking somehow.

So it was that we stayed on to teach them,
    what a *riata* and spade-bit were for.
Besides, since the Gringos had stolen California,
    I had no reason to ride south anymore.

So when the Cariboo was crawling with miners,
    with many hungry bellies to fill,
Valenzuela and I gathered a herd,
    and pushed north up to Barkerville.

Valenzuela, now he is a Rancher;
    he will chase cows all of his life.
Me, I haul freight on this rocky goat track
    to make a home for my pretty young wife.

But this evening, I will work on a bosal;
    the new riata and mecaté are done.
On the wall of my shack, hangs the tree
    of the saddle, I will build for my son.

When my Pablo is a little bit taller,
    I will take him out hunting for strays.
In those wild benchlands west of the Fraser,
    I will teach him the Vaquero's ways.

Louis Lebourdais,
Smartest Man in the Cariboo

*A campfire tale from the Cariboo Trail
told to me long ago by one of Louis'
many descendants.*

Louis Lebourdais, that Frenchman,
was born in gay Paris,
and he's the smartest guy,
in the whole Cariboo
as you will plainly see!

Louis is a right dapper coachman,
he can't think of a thing he may lack.
He drives the Cariboo Road,
every week from Ashcroft,
to Quesnel Mouth and back.

The BX provides him good horses,
thoroughbred crosses with good leg and bone,
and his coach is a shiny red Concord.
The best rig any outfit could own!

Oh, he laughs and he sings to his horses,
as they trot down that dusty dirt track.
His six-up, keeps those big wheels a hummin',
and his traces never show slack!

A little rest at each turn-around
for family comfort, and a wee bit of fun.
Old Louis he don't ever get lonely,
With a wife at each end of the run!

Hilbert Deleeuw was on of the most respected stockmen in British Columbia. He was a dedicated 4-H leader and tireless volunteer at every event serving agriculture and youth in our area. From the time I was a little boy starting out in 4-H club, through the years my wife and I spent as leaders and as our own children grew up and completed the 4-H program, Hilbert was always there, always helping, always working. Deleeuw means lion, in all the best ways, Hilbert was a lion among men!

In Memory of Hilbert Joseph Deleeuw
September 1914 – April 26, 2000

After 86 years he's crossed the divide,
the "Lion" of the bunchgrass has made his last ride.
As we gathered together to say our good-bys,
There's family and friends with tears in their eyes.

It's certain we'll miss him, but we won't forget,
He died as he lived, without much to regret.
A cowman and rancher, giving his all.
Living the life of his choosing, right up to the call.

There's two hundred 4-H kids he taught
through the years,
Standing beside businessmen and ranchers,
fightin' back tears.
We've all gathered together, old friends and new,
For one last "tip of the hat" to Hilbert Deleeuw.

In Memory of Hilbert Joseph Deleeuw
September 1914 – April 26, 2000

Just Ten Days to Go

Just think, only ten days to go. I can't understand why everyone else isn't as excited as I am. No big extravaganza downtown, not a peep out of the media! Don't they know the first **Groundhog Day** *of the new millennium is almost here!*

Now friend I wouldn't pull your leg,
and I will not steer you wrong
Groundhog Day will be a **real big deal**,
before too very long!

Holidays based on religion,
are now politicly incorrect.
So as the new age dawns on mice and men,
they'll be outlawed I suspect.

Gumboot Season

It's gumboot time in the valley
as winter's icy grip,
softened by the western breeze,
finally starts to slip.

All the things that winter hid,
are once again laid bare.
I finally found the garden rake,
Who could have left it there?

So spring is finally on it's way,
I'm glad of that I guess.
But why does winter always leave,
my yard in such a mess?

Almost...

March, always seem to me,
to be the month of mud.
Winter's pure white veil has rotted
    away,
and left us with the crud!

There's ruts and puddles everywhere,
you can't keep a darn thing clean.
But I just keep my eye on the southern
    slopes
looking for that trace of GREEN !

45

A Rainy Day in May

It's still snowing on the summer range,
so we haven't turned the cows out yet,
and things around the home place,
are just a little wet.

My neighbors have their sprinklers on,
spraying through the rain.
My eavestrough is a waterfall,
some leaves have plugged the drain.

The fields are nice and green,
'though the sky's a little grey,
and my horses seem to like the rain,
they, run, buck and play.

The ladder is a little wobbly,
but the view is worth the climb,
and I'd rather unplug
eavestroughs,
than pack sprinklers, anytime.

Gone Fishin'

Some days are just too good to waste. So I grabbed my fishing rod and
slipped down to the river.

Several deer had left their tracks
in the wet sand by the water.
So did at least a hundred geese,
a coyote and an otter.

Beaver, heron, duck and bear,
even a raccoon's tiny hand,
wrote a bit of their life's tale,
by the water in the sand.

Of course I also left my gumboot tracks,
on a day too fine to waste.
Tomorrow I'll have work to do
today I have no haste,
to end a day that is flavored as fine,
as these trout are going to taste!

Tension

June arrives with clear blue skies,
skinned knuckles and some pain,
from repairing idle machinery—
it's almost haying time again!

Changing oil and greasing tractors,
replacing broken sickle knives.
It's a trying time for farmers
but worse on farmers' wives.

For once everything is ready
I'll pace the floor again,
impatient, grim and moody,
as once more comes **The Rain.**

I Ain't Scared o' No Bugs

Written in May 1999, seven months before the big non-event. While the media was full of dire predictions about what might happen, I came up with a fool proof, environmentally friendly way to control this pest.

I checked the clock on my computer,
when I started it today.
The darn thing thinks it's February
instead of the end of May.
Suddenly it dawned on me,
Like a bolt from out fox the blue!
Saving the world from Y2K,
was simple thing to do.
I won't replace no batteries,
Or reset the VCR
Let every clock pick its own time,
like the one in my old car.
So when Two Thousand rolls around,
I'll never even know.
And I can use my old computer,
another year or so!

December 31, 1999
(The Big Countdown)

Wow! This is my last story of the milen...milleminu...millino...ah heck it's New Year's Eve and I ain't gonna waste any more time worrying about some bug whose name I can't even spell.

It will be the biggest party in a thousand years,
with fire works and champagne!
Around the world we'll celebrate,
and sing that "Auld" refrain.

Now Ma and I don't party much,
but it's a special time you see.
So we'll probably pour a little drink,
as we watch it on TV.

When the clock comes 'round to midnight,
my Darlin' and I will raise a cup,
and wave the flyswatters we gave each other,
just in case that BUG shows up.

Roadkill on the Information Highway

I waited until after all the y2whatever bugs was supposed to be squashed then I broke down and bought a new computer. I wanted to upgrade my old one but they told me it had just enough memory to make a good boat anchor.

Now I've been trying to surf the world wide web,
but I keep on fallin' in.
Everything I've tried to write,
is in the trash recycle bin.
Young Billy Gates claims this new rig,
has all the bells and whistles.
But like a spooky colt,
it bogs its head,
and I wind up in the thistles.

I used to have a real good dog,
It took me a year to learn to get out
of his way
so he could show me how smart he was.
This computer could learn a lot
from that dog.

Recently a beer commercial disguised as a strident patriotic rant, got a lot of attention from the Canadian press and the general public.

I am Canadian? OK it makes a good beer commercial but there is no need to get obnoxious about it. After all that wouldn't be very Canadian, and it is probably best that most Americans don't have a clue what we're about anyway! We share a common history and heritage and Canadians have always influenced the artistic and cultural heritage of the USA, far more than most people would ever guess. On the business side we have always endeavored to keep a low profile, after all the only foreigners who own more of the USA than the Japanese do, is us!

Quietly Canadian

We started in the fur trade days,
but most Americans don't have a clue.
Why them trappers' gatherings,
was called a Rendezvous!
Will James, Bob Nolan and Lorne Greene,
were by far the best
at quietly, redefining,
the old American West.
Half of Hollywood is now owned,
by "Canadian Club"!
And Cadillac Fairview
has New York pretty much sewed up.
In the Prohibition days,
they tried to drink "Canada Dry."
We sold them a river of whiskey,
then took over on the sly.
Now Ian Tyson is still teaching them,
what the West is all about.
While Shania is getting ready,
to buy old Nashville out.
For about fifty years,
it's been a Hollywood fact,
you have to learn to speak "Canadian"
or you don't get to act!
The Eagle may have landed,
but the folks down on the farm,
know he couldn't even scratch his butt,
without a Canadian Arm!

Still Waiting in the Pumpkin Patch

Dedicated to the memory of Charles Schultz, his cartoons were a part of so many special times when our children were growing up. Gonna miss you Charlie Brown!

You know it's about the twenty-first Halloween,
Since I became a dad.
I'm thinkin' back on all the costumes,
and all the fun we've had.

Two decades of carving pumpkins,
bonfires and trick or treats.
a menagerie of merry monsters,
running rampant through the streets.

Waiting in the pumpkin patch,
by the light of a Harvest Moon,
but the Great Pumpkin never did show up,
and my kids grew up too soon.

There's something about All Hallow's Eve,
that still gives me a thrill.
My children have out grown it now,
but their old dad never will!

A Cowboy Christmas

To those who take the time to read the rhymes and ruminations of this addle-brained cowperson, Merry Christmas and Happy New Year! May your grass be long and your winter short!

As he heads in from the feed-ground,
In the first dim glow of dawn,
The rest of the family is rising,
one by one the house lights come on.
He leaves the breath-fog shrouded cattle ,
strung out eating their hay,
Frost on their backs, and his mustache,
It is a bit chilly today.
By the time he gets back to the ranch house,
things are really in gear,
little cowfolks are hollerin'
Look Dad! Santa's bin here!
Now its time for eggnog and presents,
The family in front of the tree.
So here's wishin' a good cowboy Christmas,
To you, from my family and me!

Christmas Wish 1999

Joy, Hope and Peace on Earth,
Can't be purchased in a mall.
And there's really just one Christmas gift,
that matters after all.

So I wish you all the very best.
Have a joyous Christmas day,
as we celebrate the birth of Him,
Who came to show the way.

Because that's what it's really all about,
When all is said and done!
"For God so loved the world,"
that he gave His only Son!

Merry Christmas every one!

True Love

Two o'clock in the morning, another restless night, should be sleeping, but I need to write... The radio played that horrible song, about murder and mayhem and a love gone wrong. Some truck driving fool drove his rig through the wall...The rest of the lyrics I don't recall. Disgusted I turned the radio off and wrote this poem.

The hardest lesson in life to learn,
is simply how to love.
For most human beings,
who use the word,
don't know what they're speaking of!

For true love,
needs not to possess,
only greed and lust do that,
and love,
can never turn to hate,
in a jealous rage or spat!

True love grows from deep within,
and asks nothing in return.
It cannot die, it does not fade.
It's something you can't buy or earn.

For mortal man it's rare indeed,
to bury selfishness and pride.
To truly love, not possess or own
casting all but love aside.
Through the ages, one example,
Stands alone and shining true
Of a love so great, He gave His life
on the cross, for me and you!

Home From Winter Range

We gathered the winter range today,
and brought the cattle in.
The old cows still were fat as hogs,
but the two-year-olds were thin.
It's sixteen miles of downhill road,
and the cows all know the way
They're tired of eating slough-grass,
and looking forward to some hay.

A cattle drive in January,
ain't generally so nice.
But today the sun shone brightly,
on our world of snow and ice.
An easy day for horse and man,
because, as all cowboys know,
it ain't too hard to chase a cow,
some place she wants to go!

Retired

This poem was written for my father-in-law and a group of his co-workers on their retirement from the sawmill where they had spent so many years.

Freedom is a goal,
to which we all aspire,
Yet so many tend to panic,
when the time comes to retire.

After all those years of working hard,
in bitter cold or blazing sun,
It's time to let some other guy,
make that sawmill run.

Think of all that you can do,
now that you are free.
You can spend your days a fishin'
or watch Suzuki on TV.

You could sail across the ocean,
and around New Zealand twice.
Or spend your winters golfing,
I hear, Palm Springs is nice.

And if somehow you get too bored,
with travel, boat and putter.
Now that the forest trade,
is not your bread and butter.

If you want a change of pace,
and something new to do,
You can always call up Greenpeace,
they'll find a sign for you!

For Robert, Gary, and John, on their retirement.

Try

A cowboy never asks for much,
he just wants a chance to try.
To live, love and chase his dreams,
beneath the western sky.
It ain't just the job they choose to do,
'cause them that make a *Hand,*
are answering a call from deep inside
—they were born to ride this land.
On the range or in the arena,
it takes a special sort of man,
to ignore the storm, turn into the wind,
and do the best he can.
A cowboy will not always win,
he knows that from the start.
But every time he nods his head,
he *tries,*
with all his heart!